# Let's Talk About
# BEING BULLIED

# Let's Talk About
# BEING BULLIED

### By JOY BERRY

*Illustrated by John Costanza*
*Edited by Kate Dickey*
*Designed by Abigail Johnston*

GROLIER ENTERPRISES CORP.

Let's talk about BEING BULLIED.

A bully is a person who acts tough and likes to fight.

Bullies like to frighten or hurt people who are smaller or weaker than they are.

Some people become bullies because they *feel inferior*. They do not feel that they are as good as other people.

Bullies act as if they are big and strong to try to prove that they are as good **as** or better than other people.

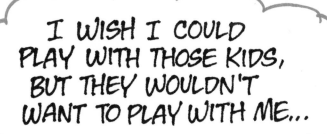

Some people become bullies because they *need attention.* They need to have people notice them.

Bullies act tough and fight so that people will notice them.

Some people become bullies because they *are frightened.* They are afraid that other people are going to hurt them.

Bullies act big and strong so that people will be afraid of them and will not bother them.

Some people become bullies because they *are angry*. Something has upset them, and they want to show that they are angry.

Bullies express their anger by being mean and by fighting with other people.

Bullies often try to control the people around them. They try to frighten other people into doing things.

When someone frightens you into doing something, you are BEING BULLIED.

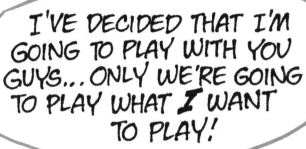

If you are like most people, you do not want to be bullied. Being bullied can upset you and make you angry.

There are several things you can do if you do not want to be bullied.

Treat bullies the same way you treat other people. *Be kind to them.*

Most people, including bullies, find it hard to be mean to a kind person. If you are kind to bullies, they may not want to bully you.

Sometimes kindness does not stop bullies.

If bullies do not respond to your kindness, *stay away from them.*

They cannot bully you if you are not around them.

Sometimes it is impossible to stay away from bullies. If you must be around bullies, *ignore them.*

Do not look at them. Do not listen to them. Do not respond to them.

They cannot bully you if you do not pay attention to them.

Sometimes it is difficult to ignore bullies.
If you cannot ignore bullies, *confront them.*

Face them. Look into their eyes. Tell them
that you do not want to be bullied.
Ask them to leave you alone.

When bullies insist on fighting, *walk or run away from them.*

They cannot fight with you if you are not there to fight.

If bullies keep bothering you, *get help*.

Talk to an adult. It could be a parent, teacher, or baby sitter. Ask the adult to help you handle the bullies who are bothering you.

No one likes being bullied. You can avoid being bullied by handling bullies in the right way. It is up to you.